Wake Up to the World of Science

OUR COASTS

B. Bornancin

Burke Books ▶ LONDON＊TORONTO＊NEW YORK

First published in the English language 1984
© Burke Publishing Company Limited 1984
Translated and adapted from *Paysages Marins*
© Editions Fernand Nathan 1984

Acknowledgements
The publishers are grateful to Anne-Elise and Robert D. Martin for preparing the text of this edition, and to the following for permission to reproduce copyright illustrations:
   Barbot; Bornancin; Cedri; Chaumeton; Fiore; Jacana: Champroux; Keller; Koch; Labat; Nathan: Beaujard; Pitch; Quéméré; Rapho; Black Star; Rives; Sester; Sygma; Vienne-Bel.
The cover illustration of *Explorer* is reproduced by permission of Salou.

AUTHOR'S NOTE

Whether you live close to the sea or far away, in a town or out in the country, you can use this book to take part in a voyage of discovery of little-known scenery, of hidden wonders, and of a surprising richness that is now under threat. If you have the chance to spend a few days at the seaside, stop and look carefully at the massive expanse of water stretching away from the coast to the horizon. Try to imagine what lies beneath the water's surface. Do you really know what is meant by the word "sea"?

CIP data
   Our coasts. – (Wake up to the world of science)
   1. Seashore biology
   I. Bornancin, B.
   II. Paysages marins. *English* III. Series
   574.941 QH137
   ISBN 0 222 01046 0
   ISBN 0 222 01047 9 Pbk

Burke Publishing Company Limited
Pegasus House, 116–120 Golden Lane, London EC1Y 0TL, England.
Burke Publishing (Canada) Limited
Registered Office: 20 Queen Street West, Suite 3000, Box 30, Toronto, Canada M5H 1V5.
Burke Publishing Company Inc.
Registered Office: 333 State Street, PO Box 1740 Bridgeport, Connecticut 06601, U.S.A.
Filmset in "Monophoto" Souvenir by Green Gates Studios, Hull, England.
Printed in the Netherlands by Deltaprint Holland.

CONTENTS

Page

All kinds of scenery

A sandy shore (Les Landes, France)

The continents are surrounded by huge areas of sea, and the long stretches of coastline provide a great variety of scenery.

Hard rocks, such as granite and limestone, are worn away by the pounding action of the sea, while pebbles and sand are continuously rolled by the waves.

If you want to walk along the seashore, always remember the following advice:

> — Never go off alone.
> — Do not forget your sandals.
> — Watch out for the waves.
> — Find out the times of the tides.

When you are travelling close to the seaside, try to take your own photographs or make a collection of postcards. Or else you can simply cut photographs out of magazines. Once you have a fairly good collection, draw a map (using an atlas for reference), mark on it the places that you have visited and glue your pictures around the map, or in a scrapbook or album.

The chalk cliffs of Dover (England)

The sea is always on the move!

A beach in Brittany (France).   **a**. at 2.00 p.m.   **b**. at 6.00 p.m.

A sandy Mediterranean shore, seen on a calm day.   **c**. at 9.00 a.m.   **d**. at 3.00 p.m.

1. By comparing photographs **a** and **b**, try to work out where the sea was at midday.

2. Look carefully at the boat and the rubber tyre in photographs **c** and **d**. Was the beach uncovered at some time between the two photographs? If so, how much of the beach was uncovered? Is it true to say that there is no tide in the Mediterranean Sea?

A wave arrives

The wave arrives . . .

. . . and retreats

The boundary between the land and the sea is a zone of continual change. Rocks and sand are submerged to varying degrees and both are pounded by the waves.

Nevertheless, seaweeds and certain kinds of animals are able to survive under these difficult conditions. You can find a variety of living things, even under rocks like those shown here, which seem to be completely bare.

The red pencil shows the scale

3. What do you notice in comparing these photographs?

Taking a closer look

a. A rocky, limestone coast bordering the Mediterranean Sea

b. A close-up view of the same coast

c. Green seaweed

On a rocky, limestone coast bordering the Mediterranean Sea, a closer look reveals zones of different coloration produced by green and brown seaweed, by seaweed that is almost black and by white or pink seaweed. Among the fronds of the seaweed you can find various animals such as limpets (**d**).

Along the lower edge of the rocks, there is a veritable underwater garden for you to explore. It provides a home for hundreds of different kinds (species) of animals.

4. Look at the dark line in photographs **a** and **b**. What do you think it means?

d. Limpets

The shore at low tide

a A muddy estuary

b. The sand exposed

At low tide, a variety of different scenes can be found along the coast: a muddy estuary (**a**), a sandy beach (**b**), and a rocky shore (**c**).

If you walk along a rocky shoreline at low tide, you will find that as the water retreats it exposes seaweed. The seaweed attached high up on the rocks (**e**) is the first to be uncovered and it is exposed for some considerable time between high tides. This seaweed is therefore well adapted to resist the effects of the sun's rays and to withstand their drying influence.

Lower down on the rocks, you will see other seaweed that is only exposed to a limited extent. As a result, successive levels of seaweed can be recognized, as shown in the diagram (**d**).

Among the fronds of the seaweed, numerous animals, such as winkles and crabs, take refuge. The bigger strands of seaweed can themselves provide a base for a whole population of attached animals (**g**).

c. A rocky coast near Roscoff (France)

e. The bladder-wrack (used as a fertilizer in some areas)

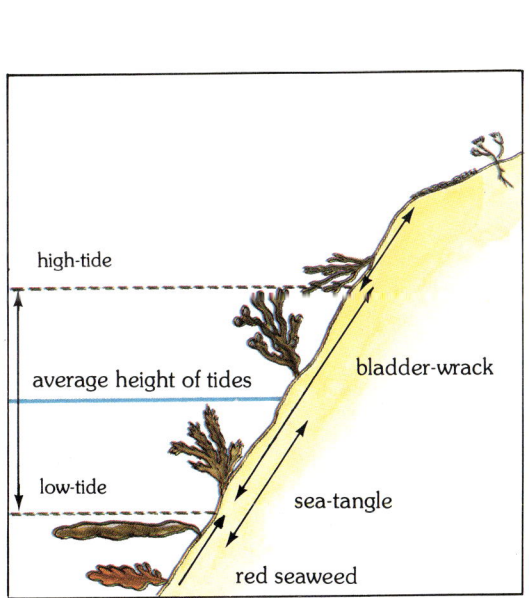

d. Successive levels of seaweed

high-tide

average height of tides

bladder-wrack

low-tide

sea-tangle

red seaweed

f. This seaweed, known as sea-tangle, is only exposed by really low tides

g. Animals attached to seaweed (colony-living polyps of the genus *Obelia*)

5. Look at photographs **a**, **b** and **c**. Which kind of shore has the most abundant growth of seaweed?

6. Compare these seaweeds with those found on the coasts of the Mediterranean (*see page* 7).

Unusual plants: seaweeds

Now that you have seen seaweeds in their natural surroundings, you can learn more about them.

How are they constructed?

Look carefully at some bunches of seaweed. There are no stems, no roots, no leaves and no veins. They simply consist of coloured sheets, filaments, ribbons, tubes or even crust-like layers that are attached to rocks by tiny suckers, holdfasts, binding threads and the like. Seaweeds are classified into basic groups according to their colour (green, brown, red, etc.); but this is not always as easy as it sounds.

How do they live?

Like all other plants, seaweeds need **water** (*see pages* 6 *and* 9) and warm conditions. In common with land-living green plants, they are able to absorb light and discharge oxygen, which is in its turn needed for the respiration of sea animals.

Light

Some seaweeds need a great deal of sunlight. They are therefore found living close to the high-tide mark and may even occur in pools. As a result, they are also adapted to withstand quite high temperatures. One example is the seaweed known as peacock's tail (**a**).

Other seaweeds grow in shady conditions, at greater depths, in rock crevices or in cave mouths.

Heat

In the Mediterranean Sea, where the water is relatively warm—with temperatures ranging from 12°C (54°F) in winter to 28°C (82°F) in summer in sheltered inlets— there are many seaweeds that contain calcium salts, such as the coralline seaweed shown in photograph **b**. They either have a hard shell or possess stiff filaments strengthened by calcium (*see photograph* **c**, *page* 7). Along the edge of the shore, these seaweeds form a kind of pavement about 1 metre (3 feet) in depth.

Seaweeds change their appearance with the season. For example, tubular green seaweeds of the genus *Enteromorpha* (**c**) are well developed in summer but die back in winter, while the corrageen moss (*Chondrus*) is red in winter (**d**) and green in summer (**e**).

Water Quality

Some kinds of seaweed require extremely **clean water**, while others can adapt to mild degrees of pollution (e.g. the sea lettuce, **f**).

Cloudy water reduces the penetration of light and the development of the seaweed is therefore limited.

7. Make a drawing of a seaweed, identify its main parts and explain how it lives.

a

b

c

d

e

f

Making a seaweed display

Find a metal or plastic container of suitable size (**a**) and pour in enough water (**b**) to give a depth of about 2 cm (1 in). Now place in the water one of the seaweeds that you have collected (**c**). Slip a piece of Bristol-board (**d**) supported by a pane of glass (**e**) beneath the seaweed to support it. Then spread out the seaweed over the board, using a knitting-needle. After you have done this, carefully lift the pane of glass so as to remove the board and the seaweed from the water. Cover the seaweed with a piece of fine material (such as a nylon stocking) and dry out the whole thing in a press.

Once your seaweeds are dry, you can set them out in an attractive display (*see page* 12).

Look at the fine display below made from **diatoms**—microscopic planktonic algae that are less than 0.1 mm ($\frac{1}{250}$ in.) in diameter. Each diatom is surrounded by a tough, finely sculptured shell.

Life in the sea

Recent advances in diving techniques have made it possible for us to learn many of the details of underwater life. With individual breathing equipment, a diver can remain under water for quite long periods of time, while his diving suit provides protection from the cold. He can also take along special apparatus to improve observation conditions.

The most striking thing as you descend into the sea is the fact that it progressively becomes darker. The "white" daylight which permits us to see on dry land is, in fact, composed of a mixture of colours, as can be seen in a rainbow. In water, however, red light is absorbed in the top 5 metres (15 feet) of the sea surface; so no red light can be seen at greater depths. At a depth of 15 metres (45 feet), green light has disappeared as well and only blue light is left. By a depth of 50 metres (150 feet) below the surface, conditions are really quite dim and there is complete darkness at depths greater than 150 metres (450 feet).

a　　　　　　　　　　　　　　　　　　　　　b

At a depth of 5 metres (15 feet), notice the difference in the range of visible colours (**a**) without and (**b**) with additional illumination.

At a depth of 1 to 25 metres (3 to 75 feet), the diver encounters a vast prairie of grass-like plants at the foot of a cliff (*see facing page*).

The diver may sometimes make unexpected discoveries, such as this cave (**d**) lying 10 metres (30 feet) below the surface. Such caves contain stalactites and stalagmites, just like those found in caves on dry land, and sometimes there are even traces of prehistoric people.

At a depth of 50 metres (150 feet), the animals found on the sandy sea-bed (**g**) are largely confined to a few flat sea-urchins.

Divers cannot go down beyond a depth of 100 metres (300 feet) unless they have a special submersible observation chamber (called a bathysphere).

8. Do you know why this cave (**d**) is under water?
9. What happens when divers switch on their lamps?
10. What can you tell from the arrangement of the fronds of these underwater plants?
11. Compare photographs **c** and **g** and try to explain the disappearance of the plants below a certain level.
12. What features of underwater life can you discover here?

c

d

e

f

g

Underwater prairies

a

Along all coastlines, stretching from the surface down to depths of 15 or 25 metres (45 or 75 feet), depending on the species concerned, there are remarkable prairies of underwater plants (**a**).

Underwater plants

The plants forming these prairies are generally known as eelgrass (*Zostera*), while in the Mediterranean Sea there are great beds of the plant *Posidonia*, which owes its scientific name to the Greek sea-god Poseidon. These plants form a dense prairie that may be as much as 1 metre (3 feet) in height. Thousands of individual fronds can be counted in each square metre (10 square feet). The fronds are regularly replaced and the old, shed fronds are washed up on the beach. Particularly in autumn, when the currents are stronger, these shed fronds tend to pile up on the beach, **b**. Along the Atlantic coast of Europe, eel-grass is collected at low tide, mixed with seaweeds, and used as a fertilizer.

b

c

If these underwater plants are examined on the spot, it is found that they are attached to the sea-bed by stout rhizomes (elongated buried stems) that resemble those of irises but grow only a few centimetres (1 or 2 inches) a year. Although it is not a regular occurrence, these plants will flower and then produce fruits (**c**) and seeds from time to time.

d

The importance of the prairie plants:

They release enormous quantities of oxygen needed by animals for respiration. Every square metre (10 square feet) of prairie produces 10 litres (18 pints) of oxygen a day; twice as much as is produced by the same area of tropical rain-forest! This supply of oxygen is of great importance, especially in bays and inlets where there is relatively shallow, calm water.

They act as egg-laying sites and as a general refuge for many animals (**d**), some of which become firmly attached to the plants (**f**).

They consolidate the sand of the sea-bed, because of their resistant, far-reaching rhizomes (**e**). They prevent the erosion of the sea-bed by currents for this reason, and this in turn provides protection for the beaches and shores.

They produce a large number of leaves that decompose naturally, thus enriching the sea with materials which can be utilized by other plants and animals.

13 Using the photograph **d** as a guide, explain the importance of the underwater prairie for animal life.

14. Can you spot the link between photographs **a** and **b**?

e

f

Is this a garden?

a. An extraordinary garden?

b. Underwater branches?

c. An underwater flower-bed?

a. A scene at a depth of 25 metres (75 feet); a rocky bed with sea-fans (gorgonians), sponges and calcium-fortified seaweeds.

b. At a depth of 40 metres (120 feet), this red "branch" attached to the white "trunk" of a sea-fan is a colony of "dead man's fingers". In both cases, you can see small polyps that regularly spread out their tentacles in the water. Each individual polyp looks rather like a sea-anemone.

c. At a depth of 15 metres (45 feet); a red coral with its polyps spread out accompanied by "animal flowers" with fine tentacles.

Peculiar animals

a. A jug with a tap?

b. Transparent tubes?

c. Underwater lace?

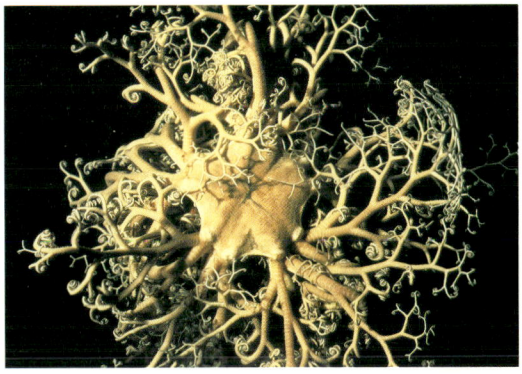

d. Tangled threads?

a. 6 metres (18 feet) below the surface sits an individual sea-squirt (*Halocynthia*)

b. At a depth of 25 metres (75 feet), this is a colony of sea-squirts (ascidians)

c. Just 20 metres (60 feet) below the surface, this piece of "Neptune's lace" is in fact a colony of tiny animals (bryozoans)

d. 60 metres (180 feet) down in the sea, a strange-looking brittle-star—a relative of the starfish

e. At a depth of 10 metres (30 feet), a feathery colony of hydroids (*Aglaophenia*). The rounded "purses" are the reproductive organs

e. Feathers?

Remarkable fish

a

b

c

d

Hide-and-seek

a. A goby has concealed itself among the pebbles of the sea-bed. This fish is able to attach itself to stones or to seaweed by means of a sucker. Note the flattened head and the large eyes

b. Is it easy to spot a flatfish (sole or flounder) on a sandy sea-bed?

c. A grey scorpion-fish resembles a rock lying amidst the seaweed, with a colony of sea-fans near by

d. A conger-eel keeps watch from the entrance to its lair among the rocks

Make drawings of these fish and their surroundings and then colour them. What do you notice?

Ceremonial Dress

Even with a single kind (species) of fish, the colour pattern can change according to sex, age, season and surroundings

e.   This photograph shows a group of rainbow wrasse. During the breeding season, the male is brilliantly coloured

f.   A John Dory, with a striking black circle on each of its silvery flanks, seen here swimming along close to the sea-bed

g.   This red gurnet has an ugly, flattened head, but it makes quite a tasty dish!

Polluting the water

a

b

c

A sewer opening into the sea

These photographs were taken near a large Mediterranean seaside town. Whenever the mistral (a strong, dry north-west wind) blows, it is easy to see the trail of dirty water marking the outlets of sewers into the sea (**a**). From the cliffs above, it is even possible to recognize a disagreeable smell rising from the sea.

d

Closer to the shore, a carpet of floating refuse can be seen (**b**). A diver would find on the sea-bed scattered bits of rubbish alongside a few sea-urchins (**c**) and patches of remaining seaweed. The underwater prairie, the marine pastureland, that once prospered in this region has died away almost completely (**d**). Compare it with the photograph on page 16.

Detergents contained in waste water discharged into the sea have attacked the underwater plants like herbicide.

Chemical analysis of the water reveals the presence of many toxic (poisonous) substances (mercury, lead, arsenic, etc.) along with a thriving population of germs. As a result, animals such as oysters that filter sea-water to extract plankton as food can become poisonous for the people who eat them.

Tar on the beaches and in the sea

Cleaning tar from your feet or from your swimsuit is no fun at all. The tar comes from ships, particularly from oil-tankers that wash out their holds at sea (**e**). The oil spreads out as a very thin layer on the water surface, cutting out some of the light, destroying plankton and poisoning animals. When the oil layer evaporates, it leaves behind heavy residues which are either washed up along the coast or deposited on the sea-bed.

e

f

From time to time, an oil-tanker sinks and the resulting oil-slick not only fouls beaches and rocks but also endangers animal life (**f**).

> The oceans of the world are threatened with death by suffocation.
> Alarm signals can now be seen clearly throughout the world.

16. Why do animals disappear when the underwater prairie dies back? (*see page* 16)

17. Mr. Smith lives 500 kilometres (300 miles) away from the sea. Where does the dirty water finish up when he washes his car alongside a stream?

18. Find out as much as you can about the various causes of sea-water pollution.

Altering the coast

The effects of industry

The combined pressures of human population increase, technological progress and industrial expansion have led to the development of coastal regions and of ports (some of which were originally fishing villages). New oil terminals are being constructed all the time and nuclear power stations are increasing in number too. Both developments involve the local expansion of service industries.

a.   A nuclear power station in Salem (United States) provides energy . . . and jobs

The effects of tourism

In a major tourist region, holidaymakers arrive in large numbers during the summer and the population can increase to three times its normal size!

   This flood of holiday visitors poses enormous problems of accommodation, food and public health. The area must be provided with extra buildings, camping-sites, shopping facilities, roads, car-parks and moorings for boats (**b**). Additional space is provided at the expense of the sea; and artificial, crescent-shaped beaches are established (**d**). As a result, the prairies beneath the waves are largely destroyed (**c**). Changes made above the water-line are achieved only at the cost of damaging the underwater environment!

   The coastline becomes completely altered as a result of these pressures from tourism and industry. But we cannot go on for ever expanding developments on land at the expense of the sea.

b. A modern marina

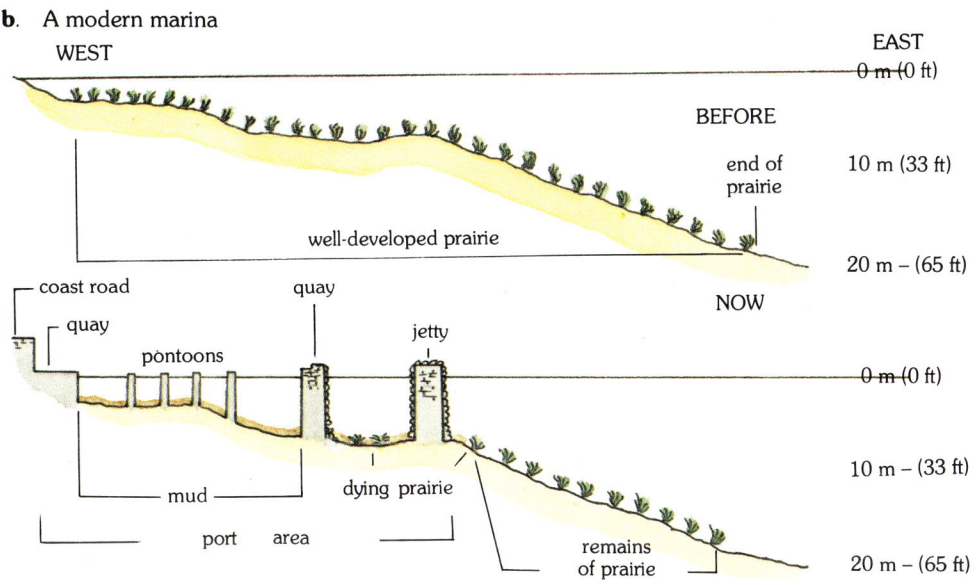

WEST

BEFORE

WELL-DEVELOPED PRAIRIE

EAST

0 m (0 ft)

end of prairie — 10 m (33 ft)

20 m – (65 ft)

coast road

quay

NOW

0 m (0 ft)

quay

pontoons

jetty

mud

dying prairie

10 m – (33 ft)

port area

remains of prairie

20 m – (65 ft)

c. The evolution of the underwater prairie beneath the marina

d. An artificial beach at a popular holiday resort

Saving the sea

Right back to prehistoric times, human beings have relied upon fish and shellfish from the sea as a source of food. In recent years, we have also learned that the sea is a major source of oxygen (generating 80 per cent of the oxygen in the atmosphere) and of drinking water. (Cloud-formation is heavily dependent upon evaporation of water from the oceans.) Planktonic algae and other marine plants produce oxygen which is dispersed by currents and thus provides a basis for animal life throughout the oceans of the world. This is a superb example of natural balance.

The sea has always been a "natural dustbin" as well, with a continuing inflow of muddy water, animal waste and even carcases. Yet such natural waste-products were easily "digested" by the sea. Everything was held in balance in a finely-tuned natural system.

But, for the last 200 years, the artificial waste generated by human activity has been accumulating into a gigantic burden which has disrupted the natural balance and threatens marine life throughout the world.

Human beings are part of nature. **If they destroy the natural environment, they destroy themselves.**

a

1. Filtering for large impurities.
2. Filtering for sand.
3. Floating oil and grease to the surface.
4. Adding chemicals to precipitate impurities dissolved in the water.
5. Allowing impurities to settle and sink to the bottom.
6. Disinfecting.

b. Cleaning a beach which has been polluted by an oil-slick

Some examples of the struggle against pollution

Only when the sea becomes clean again will we be able to breathe easily.

People have now woken up to the fact that the seas must be protected. Sea reserves were created in the United States in 1934 and Japan soon followed suit. In 1963, Europe saw the establishment of a Mediterranean reserve in the shape of the National Park of Port-Cros, just offshore from Toulon (France). Other nature reserves have been set up at sites of special interest in the Mediterranean, including one in Corsica. Plans are also afoot to create a reserve in the English Channel.

c. A protected species: The fan mussel, a large shellfish measuring up to 60 cm (24 in) across, which was at one stage on the verge of extinction

d. A diver replanting an underwater prairie

How to be a friend of the sea

29

Answers to questions

1. At midday, the rocks on the left of the photograph must have been covered by the sea, since seaweed exposed at low tide is repeatedly submerged by the tides (*see pages 6 and 8*). There are two high tides a day, alternating with low tides. The gravitational attraction forces of the sun and the moon are responsible for tides, and tidal movements are greatest at the time of the full moon.

2. The beach has been exposed along a thin strip about as wide as a car tyre. Thus, there are tidal movements in the Mediterranean, but they are so small that they can pass unnoticed if the wind is strong enough to whip up the waves.

Discovering the coasts

3. Small green and red seaweeds are solidly attached to the rocks, but they do not grow in places that are not regularly covered by sea-water. Hence, the growth of seaweeds is limited to the "level of average wave coverage". Like all other plants, seaweeds are unable to live without water.

4. The black line is irregular and it disappears beneath the rock in the photograph **b**, where there is more shade. In shaded places, there is less evaporation of water and seaweeds are able to develop better.

At low tide

5. There are no seaweeds where the sea-bed is muddy and few where it is sandy; they grow best on rocky shores.

6. In the ocean, seaweeds are larger in size than in the Mediterranean Sea.

Seaweeds

7.

Bladder-wrack in summer
(common along Atlantic coasts and
on the shores of the English Channel)

The seaweed *Cystoseira*
(common in the Mediterranean Sea)

Seaweeds absorb all the water and salts they require as nutrients directly through the surfaces of their fronds.

Beneath the waves

8. The cave was formed when the rocks were above water-level and prehistoric people were able to use it as a shelter. At a later date, the water-level rose. (When the climate was very cold at various times in the past million years, enormous glaciers locked up a great deal of water as ice, and sea-levels were generally much lower.)

9. When the powerful white light of the lamps lights up the coral, it appears red in colour because there is now sufficient light to reveal its true colour. Beforehand, everything appeared to be blue because of the effects of absorption of sunlight by the sea-water.

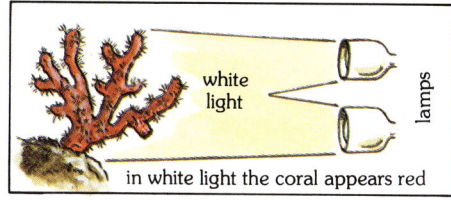

in white light the coral appears red

10. The pattern of the fronds betrays the presence of a sea-current.

11. Plants disappear when the available light is insufficient. Light is essential for the life-processes of all green plants. At a depth of 20 metres (60 feet) only 5 per cent of the sunlight arriving at the surface is still available for plants.

12. It is possible to see a gradual reduction of light in the water, the form of the underwater landscape, and the presence of marine currents.

Other factors also influence marine organisms, such as the temperature and composition of the water (*see page* 10).

Underwater prairies

13. Fish (rainbow wrasse) have come to breed; a starfish is hiding from view. The small spots on the leaves and the feather-like structures are actually colonies of small animals attached to the plants.

14. The dry fronds shown in photograph **b** come from an offshore prairie like that shown in photograph **a**.

Surprises beneath the waves

15. Animals differ from plants primarily in the manner in which they obtain their food. All animals feed on other living organisms. Green plants and algae, such as seaweeds, obtain their food from the physical environment (water, salts, etc.).

Spoiling the sea

16. Sea-living plants provide shelter for a rich animal population. If the plants are destroyed, the animals that depend upon them must also disappear.

17. The waste water runs into the stream, then into a small river, then into a larger river and then finally reaches the sea.

18. The causes of sea pollution:

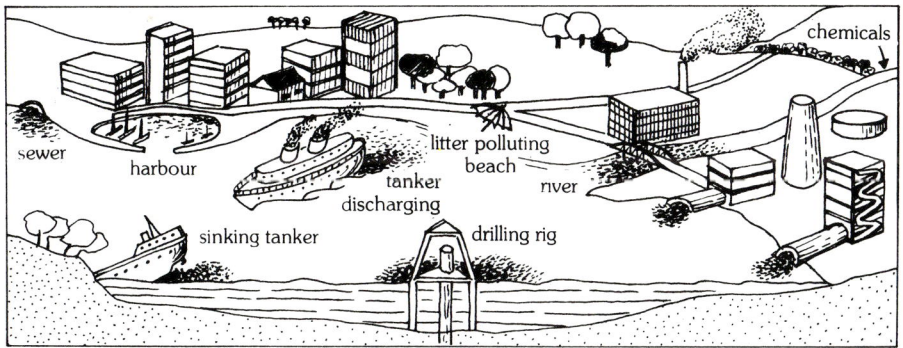

INDEX